Original title:
Island Getaway

Copyright © 2025 Creative Arts Management OÜ
All rights reserved.

Author: Oliver Bennett
ISBN HARDBACK: 978-1-80581-579-2
ISBN PAPERBACK: 978-1-80581-106-0
ISBN EBOOK: 978-1-80581-579-2

Sunrise Promises and Coconut Lullabies

The sun creeps up, the shadows flee,
My flip-flops squeak, just wait for me!
With coffee strong, I brave the sand,
And hope the seagulls understand.

A quick dip in the waves so blue,
I swear I saw a mermaid too!
But turns out it's just a flippered man,
Who's practicing his awkward tan.

Let's build a castle made of dreams,
With moats of water and silly screams.
We'll crown it high with empty cans,
And laugh while dodging beach volleyball fans.

As night falls down, we dance at ease,
I trip on sand, but hey, who sees?
With coconut snacks and laughter loud,
Together we are wacky and proud.

Crosscurrents of the Heart

In a hammock sway, I munch on chips,
While dodging ants with tiny grips.
The breeze laughs as I sip my drink,
How did I end up on this brink?

The crabs parade with sideways flair,
Unbothered, they snatch snacks with care.
I join their march, it feels just right,
As palm trees sway in evening light.

A surfboard waits, just out of reach,
Maybe I'll surf, or just take a screech!
"Help!" I shout, as I tumble 'round,
A fishy giggle at my misbound.

With fireflies dancing, stars aglow,
I ponder life, where would we go?
A heart so light, no need for maps,
Just good vibes, laughter, and coconut taps.

Whispers of the Tides

The waves came in with a funny dance,
They slipped on sand, gave toes a prance.
A seagull sneezed, the sun gave a wink,
I laughed so hard, I spilled my drink.

The crabs all marched in a little line,
Wearing sunglasses, looking quite fine.
One tipped his hat, and I thought, 'Oh me!'
Shellfish humor, as funny as can be.

Secrets Beneath the Palms

The coconuts chuckled, swaying around,
In a palm tree conference, laughter abound.
The breeze whispered jokes in a breezy tone,
While I sunbathed, feeling quite alone.

A lizard in shades strutted across,
Thought he was cool, but he looked like a boss.
I joined in his strut, we formed a parade,
Sunbaked laughter that never will fade.

Sundrenched Refuge

Under the sun, with my beach-ball grin,
I rolled in the sand, let the fun begin.
A crab called me over, said, 'Join my band!'
I tried to play tunes, but went off the strand.

We danced on the shore, an odd little crew,
With seagulls performing their own debut.
Sunblock applied, but lost in a fight,
Now I'm just a ghost, glowing in the night.

The Call of Distant Shores

I packed my bags and left with a cheer,
But forgot my shoes, oh dear, oh dear!
The sand was warm, but oh! The hot sun,
I danced like a chicken, now that's how it's done!

A fisherman laughed, 'You dance like a pro!'
'Is that your real style?' said a friend from below.
With a wink and a smile, I twirled in the mist,
Who knew a beach day could come with a twist?

The Rhythm of the Rolling Waves

The ocean's beat, it makes me sway,
A dance with crabs, in bright sun's ray.
Flip-flops fly, they take a dive,
Who knew a beach could feel so alive?

Sandy sandwiches, they stick like glue,
Seagulls steal fries, they think it's a zoo.
I'd trade my worries for a coconut drink,
But splash from a wave leaves me hard to think.

Caressed by the Evening Tide

With sunset's glow, the sky's a tease,
I trip on my towel, fall down with ease.
Laughter erupts, where no one can see,
As I wrestle the sand, it's winning me!

Chasing the crabs, they're quick little guys,
I slip and I stumble, oh what a surprise!
The stars come out, what a crazy sight,
Yet my dancing feet think it's party night!

Sheltered by the Starry Sky

Under the stars, we roast marshmallows,
But all I get is a face full of fellows.
One's got my chocolate, it's gone with a pop,
Now we're left with burnt ones; will they ever stop?

A crab's in my shorts, oh what a fright!
I dance like a fool, make it quite the sight.
The night is young, so let's raise a cheer,
For tomorrow, I'll wear a swimsuit and sneer!

A Palette of Paradise

Hula hoops flying, they're harder than thought,
Trying to show moves; forget what I wrought!
A splash here and there, I'm the star of the show,
Trying not to drown, while putting on a glow!

The drinks are bright, like a rainbow parade,
But watch out for flies, they invocate trade.
Sipping and laughing, the fun never wanes,
As my friends start a conga, in flip-flop chains!

Breeze-Kissed Breeches

A gust of wind, oh what a sight,
My trousers fly, they take to flight.
With every step, I take a chance,
My shorts do the awkward dance!

Umbrellas flip and sun hats spin,
Seagulls laugh, it's a wild din.
My flip-flops clash, they start to fight,
I chase them down with all my might!

Lapping Waves and Lullabies

The waves whistle tunes, a beachy hum,
I try to dance but just look dumb.
My sunscreen's smeared, a ghostly mess,
I'm a walking, talking, oily stress!

The tide pulls back, then gives a roar,
My sandwich flies, I shout, "More, more!"
A crab approaches, ready to steal,
I guess it's lunch for our crustacean meal!

Footloose on Sandy Shores

Sand between toes, life's so grand,
I trip on flip-flops—oh, what a stand!
The beach ball bounces, hits my head,
   I wonder if my brain's still fed.

With every wave, my laughter swells,
The sunburn's here, oh how it quells.
I shout for joy, though I look meek,
   Beach curls stick—it's beachy chic!

The Heartbeat of the Horizon

Sunset's glow, a pastel parade,
I trip on chords, a tune's misplayed.
The crickets chirp, a serenade,
While I fumble snacks, a mess I've made!

A dolphin jumps, I gasp in awe,
Then trip on a towel, oh what a flaw!
With laughter echoing, I take a bow,
Tomorrow's plan? I'll figure out how!

The Dance of Dawn on Saltwater

As the sun yawns wide and bright,
A crab declares his morning fight.
Seagulls chase the waves with glee,
While dolphins laugh; what a sight to see!

The beach ball rolls as kids take flight,
Landing in sand, oh what a sight!
With sunscreen in their eyes, they squint,
Their laughter rises; joy's no hint!

Fishermen throw their lines with flair,
Only to catch socks, what a scare!
The seaweed dances, all in rhyme,
While the sun keeps perfect time!

So let the waves bring tales anew,
Of fishy friends and fun for two.
As dawn breaks free from sleepy chores,
Let's jig and jump on sandy shores!

Revelry at the Edge of the World

At dusk, when colors burst and swirl,
Seashells sing, as if they twirl.
A surfboard takes a dive with flair,
And surf rats throw their locks in air!

The hammock sways, a ships' delight,
While tourists try the local bite.
A crab with swagger steals the show,
As laughter rides the tide's soft flow.

The bonfire sputters, sparks take flight,
As sandcastles begin their fight.
With buckets tossed and shovels lost,
The seagulls dive; it's fun at all costs!

Here at the edge, where skies collide,
You'll find the fish who dance with pride.
So raise a toast to ocean's cheer,
For goofy fun waits every year!

Whispers of the Ocean Breeze

Waves whisper secrets to the shore,
As laughter echoes, wanting more.
A sea sponge dons a beach hat bright,
While splash fights spark like pure delight!

The flip-flops flop in wild parade,
As sunset casts its golden shade.
With water pistols rules are bent,
A dolphin giggles, so content.

Shells are scattered, treasures old,
With stories of adventures bold.
Each grain of sand, a purpose found,
While mermaids dance in circles round.

So let the tides bring forth their jest,
Where salty air is at its best.
We'll sing and sway, embrace the tease,
In the realm of ocean breeze!

Sunlit Shores and Wandering Hearts

On sunlit shores, the flip-flops fly,
While kids build castles hoping high.
A lazy dog takes up the space,
While sunbathers enjoy their grace.

With ice cream dripping, the giggles grow,
And beach balls bounce in bright aglow.
The crabwalk dance, a clumsy show,
With laughter loud, oh how they flow!

In search of treasure, maps are drawn,
Instead, what's found? A half-eaten prawn!
But joy is rich with every find,
As wandering hearts leave worries behind.

So let the surf provide the thrill,
With each push, every wave, every chill.
For in this paradise, we're free to play,
Sunlit adventures light up our day!

Hearts Set Sail into the Horizon

We packed our bags with flip-flops tight,
And launched our dreams into the night.
The sea gulls squawked a merry tune,
While we danced under the lazy moon.

With sunscreen lathered on our nose,
We met some crabs who struck a pose.
They asked for tips on how to dance,
We laughed so hard, we lost our chance.

The boat went left, then quickly right,
We spilled our drinks, what a silly sight!
As waves crashed in with playful glee,
Our laughter echoed, wild and free.

When seagulls dive, the fun begins,
We chased our hats, the best of wins.
With salty air and hearts aflame,
Getting lost is our favorite game.

The Allure of Cloudless Skies

Up above, the sky's a tease,
With birds in shorts flying with ease.
We waved hello to monty clouds,
But they just giggled, way too proud.

On deck chairs, we tried to tan,
But ended up a lobster clan.
The snacks we brought? Oh what a plight,
Caught a seagull munching in delight.

Our drinks were swirled with silly straws,
We built a sandman with no flaws.
He wore our shades and fake mustache,
Then toppled down with one big crash.

With sunburned noses, off we glide,
The warmth of laughter, our joyride.
In paradise, where time unfolds,
The funniest of stories are always told.

Beneath the Palms, Time Stands Still

Beneath the palms, in a swaying chair,
We munch on snacks without a care.
A coconut fell, it made a thud,
We laughed so hard, then rolled in the mud.

The parrot squawked, it had some flair,
It mimicked us, what a funny affair!
It flaunted jokes with perfect timing,
We all agreed, its punchlines shining.

We tried to nap but dreams took flight,
With visions of dancing, pure delight.
A crab in shades broke out a groove,
We cheered it on, it had the move!

As shadows stretched across the sand,
We crafted castles, nothing bland.
In silly hats, our spirits soared,
In laughter's grasp, we were adored.

The Taste of Mango on Sunlit Lemons

With juicy mango dribbling down,
We wore bright smiles, our favorite crown.
Slice a lemon, mix it right,
A citrus splash, what a delight!

We tossed our worries to the seas,
Played hopscotch with some curious bees.
They buzzed along, our little crew,
And danced around like it was new.

The sun was hot, but laughter cool,
We made up games that seemed a fool.
A watermelon slip, oh what a sight,
We slid on racks, and took flight!

The taste of summer on our tongues,
With ice cream cones and silly songs.
As night approached, the stars would gleam,
In this sweet place, we lived the dream.

A Symphony of Seashells

In the sun, we found a tune,
Seashells dancing, oh so soon,
A crab joined in, with quite a flair,
Swaying snails, without a care.

Waves were clapping, what a show,
Fish in shades of rainbow glow,
Seagulls laughed, they took the lead,
Dropping snacks for all to feed.

Rhythm carried through the air,
With a twist, we boldly dare,
Mermaid laughing, splashes fly,
Dolphins giggle, soaring high.

So we tapped our toes in glee,
Shells and waves in harmony,
Life's a concert, full of fun,
On this stage, we shine like sun.

The Lure of Lush Horizons

Beneath a tree, we spread a sheet,
Fruit and laughter—a tasty treat,
Coconuts roll, what a sight,
Monkeys cheer, with pure delight.

Palm trees sway, they wave their fans,
Sunburned tourists, making plans,
Sipping drinks from silly cups,
While the sand just eats them up.

A parrot squawks, "Who's got the chips?"
As we dive in, there's laughter's grip,
Jumping waves, our courage bold,
A mermaid scoffs, "You're far too old!"

Evenings glow with stories shared,
Tales of blunders, nothing spared,
We revel under starlit skies,
With each giggle, the palm tree sighs.

Footprints in the Sand

Waking late, the sun's a tease,
Footprints leading, where's the cheese?
Sandcastles made, a royal seat,
But the tide's coming, cheers retreat!

Laughter echoes as we race,
To save our crowns, a frantic chase,
Seagulls circle, plan a heist,
Swipe a sandwich, oh so nice!

Flip-flops flying, where'd they go?
Stuck in sand, we laugh, "Oh no!"
Rolling waves bring unexpected fun,
Dried seaweed? Snack's begun!

As the sun dips low and red,
With salty skin, we head to bed,
Dreaming of our sandy plight,
In our dreams, we'll win the fight.

Tropical Reverie

In hammocks swung, we sway and swing,
Dreams as light as parrot wings,
Beneath the shade of mango trees,
We giggle loud, with full-blown ease.

Jellyfish swim in silly hats,
Feeling fancy, oh those brats,
Dance with crabs, a wiggly show,
Sand between toes—such a flow!

Laughter bubbles with each splash,
A game of tag, a silly dash,
The sun sets low, a warm embrace,
Sunburnt noses, oh what a race!

As stars appear, we tell the tales,
Of epic fails and mighty gales,
With every chuckle, hearts grow wide,
In this dreamy place, we abide.

Sunsets that Paint the Heart

The sky bursts bright with orange hues,
A seagull steals my lunch with moves.
I laugh and run, but trip on sand,
Falling hard, still feeling grand.

The sun's going down but I won't be blue,
My drink just spilled, oh what a view!
Friends around, laughter in the air,
As we pretend we haven't a care.

Awash in the Dance of Sunbeams

A hula dance gone wrong, oh dear,
I shake my hips, the crowd can hear.
The waves applaud, they seem amused,
As I trip again, oh, I'm quite confused.

Sunbeams laugh as they warm my toes,
Bikini top slips, well, that's how it goes!
Laughter erupts, oh what a sight,
Just another day under the bright sunlight.

The Symphonic Sea Serenade

The ocean sings a silly tune,
Whales join in, under the moon.
I serenade with a plastic flute,
Fish are flopping, they want to hoot.

Seagulls squawk in perfect time,
And crabs do the cha-cha, oh what a rhyme!
Sandcastles crumble with each refrain,
Yet silliness is my true domain.

Memories in a Seashell's Whisper

A shell held close, it whispers loud,
Telling tales of a sun-kissed crowd.
I chased a crab, it chased me back,
In this quirky little beachy hack.

Collecting memories with each wave,
As sunscreen drips, oh what a rave!
I laugh, I play, I dance with glee,
Crafting joy under a coconut tree.

Serenity in Salty Breezes

With flip-flops flopping by my side,
I tripped on sand and took a ride.
A seagull snatched my tasty snack,
I yelled, 'Come back!' but he won't track.

The sun is hot, my drink's all gone,
I wave my hands, a beachy con.
Laughter echoes as I fall,
Into the waves, oh what a call!

The surfboards flop, we try to stand,
My friend just wiped out, what a grand!
We build a tower, but it's a pile,
Of sand and dreams, we grin and smile.

As twilight falls, we light a fire,
With marshmallows that we all desire.
In salty breezes, we laugh till late,
With goofy tales, our hearts elate.

Hidden Havens

In a cove where crabs dance about,
We lost our map, but laugh and shout.
The coconut fell right on my head,
I think I'll just go back to bed.

Floating on noodles, we paddle close,
The fish all giggle, it's quite a dose.
With sunscreen smeared on everyone's nose,
Why do we look like clowns in clothes?

The hammock's swaying, we nap too long,
Awoken by a rooster's song.
We chase the sunset, slipping and sliding,
Two goober friends, joyfully colliding.

When night descends, the stars appear,
And bugs are buzzing, oh dear, oh dear!
We laugh it off, with drinks in hand,
In our secret spot, just blissful and tanned.

Echoes of Wave and Wind

The ocean waves go up and down,
I tried to swim, but lost my crown.
A wave came crashing, what a blast,
Now I'm soaking, but it's a laugh.

Beach ball bounces across the shore,
We dive for it, but fall once more.
A sandcastle built, but it won't last,
As seagulls circle, plotting fast.

With friends in tow, we stroll the sand,
Life feels perfect, like a band.
I trip and tumble, roll with glee,
Oh look, a crab! Just laughed at me!

As night arrives, we dance and cheer,
With fireflies buzzing, drawing near.
In echoes of laughter that won't rescind,
We share our tales 'til the night ends.

Paradise Found in Azure Dreams

A drink in hand, umbrella bright,
I sipped too fast and lost my sight.
The waves they crash, I stand up tall,
Only to stumble, doing a fall.

The sun is shining, my flip-flop's lost,
I search around, what a cost!
With giggles shared and clumsy falls,
We dive for shells while laughter calls.

We carve our names into the sand,
Only to see the tide's swift hand.
A dolphin jumps as we cheer aloud,
In this quirky place, we feel so proud.

The stars above twinkle so wide,
In this bright bliss, with friends beside.
What tales we'll tell, when we return,
In azure dreams, our hearts still yearn.

Lighthouses and Lost Trails

Upon the rocks, a beacon stands,
A guide for seas with silly hands.
I wandered off, my map in knots,
Chased crabs that laughed, abandoned thoughts.

The waves would tickle my tired feet,
While seagulls squawked a rhythmic beat.
A lighthouse keeper with a pie,
Said, "Find your way or at least try!"

My compass spins, it mocks my quest,
As sunset paints the ocean's vest.
I wave to boats, they wave back too,
Or maybe they're just laughing at you.

So here's my tale of trails unknown,
With lighthouses that have brightly shone.
I'll remember each giggling wave,
In a place where mischiefs misbehave.

Where Ocean Meets Solitude

On a beach so wide, away from the crowd,
I tried to build a tower, it fell down loud.
A crab became my architect plea,
With a judgmental glare, it walked past me.

The ocean's vast, it swayed with glee,
As I splashed my drink, like a wild spree.
A seagull swooped for a slice of bread,
And suddenly, my lunch was dead.

I chuckled at the pelicans, dressed so grand,
Who thought they owned this sandy land.
They dove for fish, I laughed and sighed,
In solitude, but with friends at my side.

As sunset drapes like a soft curtain,
The waves whisper secrets, quite uncertain.
With laughter mingled amid the blue,
I found my peace, just being a fool too.

Sunsets and Starlit Vistas

At dusk, the sun begins its show,
Painting skies a fiery glow.
I dropped my drink in awe, oh dear,
As seagulls chuckled, drawing near.

The stars appeared, a twinkling mess,
While I tried to dance, made quite a press.
Tripped over sand with grace unkind,
Laughter echoed, a fun rewind.

Romance was in the salty air,
Except for the crabs, who just don't care.
They held a meeting, plotting delight,
As I flopped around like a kite in flight.

With waves that mocked my silly fate,
I cheered them on — they always rate.
Beneath the stars, I raised a toast,
To laughter and joy, I'd gladly boast.

Coral Reflections

The reef below, a colorful grin,
As fish swam by, sporting a fin.
With goggles on, I made a scene,
Dancing like a shrimp, all shiny and keen.

A clownfish giggled as I pranced,
In coral gardens, I thought I danced.
But dodging eels with a sideways jive,
Had me thinking, 'Am I even alive?'

The waters shimmered, a funny sight,
With turtles winking as they took flight.
I lost my flippers, had to crab-crawl,
As laughter echoed, I took a fall.

In depths of blue, I learned quite fast,
That being silly is a blast!
So here's to reefs, where laughter flows,
And treasures hide where the seaweed grows.

The Canvas of an Endless Summer

Sandy toes and sunburned nose,
A drink in hand, who really knows?
The seagulls squawk, they want my fry,
As I wave goodbye with a cheesy pie.

The sunscreen's thick, it won't absorb,
My beach hat's got its own best-sorb.
A crab scuttles by with a curious stare,
"Not my lunch!" I shout, flailing in despair.

My buddy's tan is like burnt toast,
While I sport stripes and brag the most.
We laugh at all our silly flaws,
Sunburns and drinks, hey, it's the cause!

As dusk arrives, the fire's aglow,
S'Mores gone wrong? Oh no, oh no!
With friends all near and laughter loud,
This summer canvas sure makes me proud.

A Medley of Dune and Dream

On shifting sands I lost my shoe,
A rogue wave laughs, it's calling too.
The beach ball flies like a wayward kite,
While sun hats tumble, oh what a sight!

Building castles, then they crash,
The tide rolls in, a tidal splash.
With each tumble, we burst with glee,
Sand in my shorts, oh woe is me!

My buddy tries to surf for fun,
But he just flops, no battle won.
"I swear I'm the next Kelly Slater!"
He sinks like a stone, we cheer, "See you later!"

At twilight we dine on fishy delight,
"Did someone order the seaworm bite?"
With giggles and worms, we toast the night,
Our sandy adventure, oh what a fright!

Under a Canopy of Stars

Laying back on a blanket spread,
Count the stars, then count my bread.
"Is that a star or my buddy's snore?"
We laugh and agree, we need a score!

A comet zips, or was that a plane?
His wild stories start to wane.
We share ghost tales 'neath the moonlit glow,
And fight off bugs with much ado, though.

"Did you feel that?" he jumps and yells,
It's just the wind, no ghostly spells.
With flashlights buzzing, we dance in place,
Tripping over snacks, oh, what a race!

Under stars, we twist and twirl,
His dance moves make my head whirl.
Each moment shared, a funny sight,
Best night ever, 'til morning light!

Reflections in the Tide

Water glistens, I see my face,
"What happened here? Is that a trace?"
With salty hair and silly grin,
I swear that's not me, it's a jester's twin!

With each wave crashing, I jump and play,
Kicking up foam in an artful way.
A dolphin prances, does it wink at me?
"Hey buddy, stop splashing; let's have tea!"

We chase the tide, it runs away,
But we'll catch it soon, just not today.
My flip-flop's gone, just like my grace,
Sandals mix-up—oh, what a chase!

As sunset paints the sky so bright,
We strike a pose, what a silly sight!
With laughter echoing through the sand,
These memories cherished, forever planned.

Reflections on a Teal Canvas

In teal waters, thoughts drift free,
A fish once questioned my degree.
"You swim in circles, what's the plan?"
I winked and said, "I'm my own fan!"

Seagulls cackle, stealing my fries,
As I debate whether to dive or fly.
They squawk and swoop with cheeky flair,
I just hope they don't mess my hair!

The sun slips low, a warm embrace,
I lost my shoe in this sandy race.
Footprints lead to a crabby foe,
Who scuttles off as I shout, "Whoa!"

With a splash and a laugh, I'll soon forget,
This beach trip's my best goofball bet.
In teal waters under skies so bright,
Who knew relaxation could be so light?

Beneath Coconut Canopies

Beneath the trees, I start to sway,
A coconut drops, oh what a day!
I dodge and weave with flair and zest,
While the locals cheer, "You're the best!"

Mango smoothies, a brain freeze surprise,
I giggle loud, can't hold my cries.
As the waiter grins and pours more ice,
I just hope this doesn't come with a price!

Little crabs use my toes as a bridge,
I squeal and leap, it's quite the midge!
"Excuse me, folks, I'm not a toy!"
They pinch my heel – oh what a ploy!

Night falls fast, the stars are bright,
I can't stop laughing at my sunburn plight.
Beneath the trees, we dance and play,
As laughter echoes night into day.

Tides of Time and Tranquility

The waves whisper jokes from afar,
One made me laugh, then splashed my car!
With sandy cheeks and salty hair,
I'm the beach bum without a care.

A beach ball escapes in a raucous breeze,
I chase it down, but it's quite the tease.
Flip-flops flying, a comical sight,
I tumble and laugh, it feels so right!

The tide rolls in with a giggle and roar,
As seagulls plot my snack with a score.
I share my chips, what a bold move,
But friendship with birds, I strive to prove!

With sunset hues that steal the show,
I ponder how far my courage can go.
In a splash of waves, I make my stand,
With sandy toes and a giggling band!

Wanderlust by the Waters' Edge

By the water, I found a shoe,
It's not my size, but it'll do!
I strut along, a fashion queen,
With mismatched pride, what a scene!

A crab gives me its best side-eye,
I bow to it, my silly reply.
"Dear sir, your shell could use a rhyme,
Why not join me for some beachy time?"

Beach umbrellas dance in the breeze,
As sunbathers sprout like surreal trees.
Some flip and flop with watermelon glee,
While others sunbathe, snoozing carefree.

As the daylight fades and night creeps near,
I sip my drink and toast the cheer.
In the glow of laughter, I make my pledge,
To roam always by the waters' edge!

The Calm Before the Sunset

Seagulls squawk, it's time to play,
My sunscreen's missing, what a day!
A crab scuttles off with my chip,
    I'm in a race, oh let it rip!

Beach towels tossed like ships at sea,
Why does my flip-flop always flee?
Sand in my sandwich, gritty surprise,
Why does this happen? I roll my eyes.

As the sun dips low, it's glow so bright,
I drop my drink, that was not right!
Laughter echoes, waves crashing near,
    The beach is wild, full of cheer.

This funny chaos, a sight to see,
Who's to blame? Not even me!
With salty hair and a sunburned nose,
Tomorrow's fun, goodness knows!

Breezy Afternoons in the Sun

Kites above do pirouettes,
My sandwich flew, I have regrets!
A toddler's joy, my hat's now lost,
The breeze is bold, what's the cost?

Cool drinks spill like a wild stream,
Chasing seagulls, it's a dream!
Slapstick moments, laughter loud,
Sunburned and silly, I feel so proud.

Tanned legs tangled in beach twine,
That wave just said, 'Oh, you're mine!'
The sand is soft, my foot's a mess,
Wet and wild? I must confess!

Chasing my dog who thinks it's a race,
Why's he rolling? In sand? No space!
Giggles abound with each tidal sweep,
The day grows long, and I need my sleep!

Sandcastles Under a Whispering Moon

Building towers, my forte,
Oh wait, where did my bucket stray?
A dog comes near, thinks it's a snack,
With sandy bites, I'm under attack!

Night falls slow, the moon aglow,
I tripped over my own toe!
A crab in my moat? Who let him in?
Building dreams where chaos begins.

Lights from nearby echo soft shouts,
Why does my drink taste like socks? Counts!
The breeze whispers secrets, sweet and bright,
Making memories, keeping it light.

The waves applaud my towers of sand,
Oh, look, there goes my best friend's hand!
Cackling laughter under the stars,
Tonight's adventures written in scars!

Shells of Time Along the Shore

Collecting shells, a treasure chest,
Wait, this one's fuzzy? What a jest!
Each footstep etched upon the sand,
I think my flip-flops have a plan.

Sunburned smiles as we strut along,
Crabs do a dance, oh, what's wrong?
A hermit crab with attitude fierce,
Shuffling away, he loves to pierce.

Sunset fades; colors swirl like dreams,
My towel's shifting; it surely screams!
Where is my drink? Did I leave it there?
With all these laughs, I'm filled with care.

Each shell a memory I keep tight,
Finding joy in the silly plight!
Days go by like waves on the bay,
With giggles echoing, I'll always stay!

A Symphony of Seagulls and Surf

The gulls are squawking, what a sound,
They steal my chips, they're quite renowned.
Waves crash loud, they dance in glee,
While I'm just hoping for a cup of tea.

Sandy toes and sunburned nose,
The sun comes up, and off it goes.
I chased a crab, but lost the race,
He waved goodbye, with lots of grace.

Beach balls bounce, like minds gone wild,
My inner child, oh how it smiled.
Sunning here, with drink in hand,
What a life, it's simply grand!

With laughter echoing in the breeze,
The ocean whispers, "Oh, just tease!"
In this retreat, far from the rush,
I'll trade my woes for a cheeky hush.

Retreat to the Infinite Blue

Palm trees sway, with a lazy grin,
I'm here for fun, let the games begin!
The sky is bright, in hues so bold,
Who needs a map when there's sun to behold?

Ice cream drips, and so does my brain,
I sit on the sand, feeling quite vain.
A stray dog joins, thinks he belongs,
With his wagging tail and catchy songs.

Surfers tumble, splash and fall,
While I'm just happy to watch it all.
Seashells whisper, "Take us home,"
I'll leave them here, my heart will roam.

Sunset comes, the sky turns pink,
With a twinkle in my eye, I clink.
A toast to dreams, and laughter galore,
In this playful space, who could ask for more?

The Solace of Saltwater Dreams

The ocean chuckles, waves flirt and tease,
Nearby, a tourist climbs up a tree.
"I'm the king!" he shouts, what a sight,
But down he goes, he's lost the fight!

Sandcastles rise, then meet their end,
As kids attack, it's hard to defend.
With moats and flags, they lay their claim,
Then mother waves, it's time for the game.

My sunhat flies, a seagull steals,
As I chase it down, I trip on wheels!
Back again, it's laughter and cheer,
In this wild place, my worries disappear.

The stars above, begin to twinkle,
As night descends, the fireflies sprinkle.
With s'mores in hand, the stories flow,
In this sunny nook, what a show!

Twilight in Turquoise Waters

As twilight glimmers, the beach's still,
Just me and my drink, and a friendly quill.
The parrot laughs, perched on a chair,
Sipping my cocktail, without a care.

Floats in the pool, I duck and weave,
Trying to dodge, a hard reprieve.
The splashes echo, as laughter rings,
I guess tonight, we're all the kings.

Cranky crabs join the late-night dance,
While toasting pineapples, we take a chance.
With music playing, we sway and sway,
Every problem's kept at bay.

The moon beams down, a silver slice,
We share our dreams, more than once or twice.
In this laughter, every friend is dear,
As the night unfolds, we shed a tear.

Melodies of Surging Surf

Waves crash like clumsy dancers,
Seagulls squawk like they have answers.
Sand stuck to sunscreened knees,
Laughing at the ocean's tease.

Shells sing songs of ancient lore,
Beach towels spread like wings to soar.
Flip-flops fly in a gusty breeze,
Chasing crabs, oh what a tease!

Kids build castles, oh so grand,
While parents snooze, drink in hand.
A beach ball bounces with such flair,
Ending up in someone's hair!

Sunburnt noses and silly hats,
Caught in games with friendly cats.
Sandwiches lost in seagull's dive,
But oh, the fun—feel so alive!

Cascades of Colorful Coral

Underwater dance with fish so bright,
A snorkel's giggle brings pure delight.
Surfboards float like unruly dreams,
As laughter bubbles, or so it seems.

Coral reefs wave in silly tunes,
While jellyfish sport their disco balloons.
Bubbles pop, and giggles rise,
Even turtles roll their eyes.

An octopus winks with crafty style,
While divers trip and swim a mile.
The sun dips low, casting gold,
Echoing stories that must be told.

Flippers fly, making quite the splash,
A fishy face leaves a quick dash.
Crabs moonwalk with clacking claws,
Underwater parties give hearty applause!

Moonlit Nights by the Sea

Beneath the stars, the waves do sigh,
As beachcombers let out a sigh.
Lanterns flicker like fireflies,
Bringing giggles and silly ties.

Bonfire's crackle, marshmallows gleam,
Stickiness sticks, or so it would seem.
S'mores that melt like dreams took flight,
And laughter echoes into the night.

A ukulele strums a goofy tune,
As crabs dance under a beach ball moon.
Flavors of ocean mix with the sweet,
As flip-flops skip, skipping to the beat.

Starfish share their cosmic view,
While tides debate who's the best of the crew.
Sandcastles tumble in the tide's embrace,
Yet still we laugh, not a frown on our face!

Waterscapes of Dream and Dusk

With splashes bright, adventures arise,
Water fights spark with silly surprise.
Rubber ducks float, quite out of place,
While waves splash joy, the sun's warm embrace.

Kites soar high with tails aflutter,
While kids chase through the sand's warm butter.
A coconut tumbles, quite out of luck,
As giggles erupt: what's that in the muck?

Cartwheels accidently end in a fall,
Friends roll in laughter, enjoying it all.
Footprints dance on water's skin,
And oh, let the chaos gently begin!

Ice cream drips down the cone's side,
As dolphins swim with merriment and pride.
Sunsets glow in hues of cheer,
Our getaway's magic, oh so dear!

Encounters with the Curious Tide

The tide rolled in with a giggle,
Crabs danced with a little wiggle,
Seagulls squawked in silly tones,
As sandcastles fell like wooden thrones.

I met a fish with a bright pink hat,
He winked and said, "Don't step on my mat!"
The jellyfish joined the boisterous play,
Wobbling about in a clumsy ballet.

A starfish twirled like a disco queen,
While seaweed swayed in a wavy green,
Every splash held a rhyme so absurd,
Even the waves danced, it was terribly heard!

With laughter ringing across the shore,
Life here's never a bore, oh no more!
For when the tide sings its salty song,
You find that silly is where you belong.

A Gaze into Open Horizons

I laid back on the sun-warmed sand,
Staring up high, my dreams unplanned,
A cloud shaped like an ice cream cone,
Brought a chuckle in my sunbaked zone.

With a beach ball that wouldn't sit still,
Chasing it felt like a wild thrill,
A seagull swooped, my snack it eyed,
And off it flew with my fries in pride!

The horizon painted in vibrant hues,
Where laughter echoed, and fun ensues,
In this place where time tends to bend,
Every glance feels like a crazy trend.

I tossed my worries with the sea breeze,
While sipping a drink that brought me to knees,
For in the shimmer of waves and sun,
I found that laughter is always fun!

The Last Dance of the Dusk

As the sun dipped low, casting golden rays,
The beach turned into a stage for plays,
Crickets chirped in a rhythmic beat,
While the sand whispered secrets beneath my feet.

A crab in a tux, how dapper he seemed,
Twirled with a snail who fancied he dreamed,
They spun and they kicked up grains of sand,
While waves cheered loud, a clapping band!

A beach party broke out with shells as the band,
Oh, how we laughed, hand in hand,
Under the colors of a pastel sunset,
This night was one I'd never forget!

With a final shimmy and joyful cheer,
The stars peeked out, twinkling near,
As laughter faded into the night's embrace,
We all went home with smiles on our face.

Farewells Woven in Seafoam

In the mist where the blue waves froth,
I waved goodbye while wearing a cloth,
Made of seaweed, so fashionably chic,
The ocean chuckled, 'Oh, what a peek!'

The shells whispered secrets of those who'd stayed,
While crabs rolled by, with no sign of trade,
I dropped my flip-flop in a humorous slip,
And watched as the tide made off with my trip!

A fish floated by with a wink and a nod,
Claiming my towel, then said, "It's so odd!"
We shared a laugh, though I felt quite lost,
Yet the ocean ensured I could bear the cost.

As dusk turned to night, I called out a cheer,
While the frothy sea danced, no hint of a fear,
For even in farewells, there's laughter galore,
In the joyful embrace of this sandy shore.

Fables of the Forgotten Coast

With a hat too large, and shorts too tight,
They dance with crabs, oh what a sight!
Their sunscreen glistens, a ghostly glow,
While seagulls plot, in a feathered show.

The waves come crashing, like laughter's roar,
Tumbles and stumbles, who could want more?
Flip-flops flying, as they chase their drinks,
Sipping on joy, oh how it winks!

Sandcastles rise with a splashy flair,
A moat of giggles, without a care.
But tides have plans, they sneak and creep,
Destroying the fortress while they all leap!

When twilight hugs the shore so tight,
They roast marshmallows, igniting the night.
With stories bold, laughter rings clear,
A memory made, as they share a cheer!

Serenades of Solitude

Here I sit with my coconut drink,
Watching the seagulls, oh how they blink!
A straw hat bobbing, it flies off my head,
And lands on a turtle, who's probably fed.

Solitude sings in the soft ocean breeze,
While I try to find my lost car keys.
A smoothie spilled, now it's a sticky quest,
With ants who waltz, I can't help but jest!

The sun paints stripes, like a clown in a show,
And I giggle along, oh where did time go?
A hammock sways with a swish and a sway,
But I tumble and roll, what a comical day!

As stars blink above, I dance on the sand,
With shells for maracas, oh how they stand!
Those clumsy moves make me laugh till I ache,
My one-man parade, oh what fun I make!

Footprints in the Soft Earth

Barefoot and puzzled, those prints in a line,
Turtle or human? Who knows, it's fine!
Slipping and sliding, I cannot keep track,
Did I just moonwalk? Where's my cool knack?

Crabs join the fun, with their sideways prance,
They critique my moves, oh what a chance!
With seashells a-dancing, much like a show,
I end up giggling, out there in the glow.

A flip-flop flies, through the salty air,
While chasing a gull without a care.
And splashes ensue, from my clumsy feet,
I'm just a comedian, not quite discreet!

As daylight wanes and laughter renews,
I find all my footprints, in varied hues.
The ocean waves whisper, "You cracked quite a smile!"
With echoes of joy that stretch for a mile!

Between Waves and Wishes

Beneath the sun, I dream of the sea,
With wishes afloat, just like me!
I toss a coin, but it's more of a flop,
Did it land in the drink or on jellyfish top?

Seagulls dive down, what a cheeky bunch,
Claiming my fries, oh, they're out for lunch!
I flail and I squeal, "Hey, those are mine!"
They laugh and they squawk, "No need to whine!"

Surfboards wobble, like cows on a spree,
A dabble of wiggles, oh can't you see?
With a splash and a crash, into soft, salty foam,
I find myself thinking, "Is this still home?"

As night creeps in, wishes take flight,
Glow sticks and laughter illuminate the night.
Between waves and wishes, the fun's all around,
With joy in the air, it surely is found!

Secrets Beneath the Tropical Sun

A crab named Larry stole my flip-flops,
He scuttled away while I tried not to drop.
Sunburned noses and drinks that spill,
In the quest for shade, I tripped on a grill.

The locals chuckled, a sight to behold,
My towel, a cape, made me feel quite bold.
With each laugh shared, I lost track of time,
As fish showed off in perfect mime.

Seagulls squawked with a flair for the drama,
Diving for fries was their daily llama.
The sun set low, painting skies of gold,
While I questioned if I was brave or just old.

In quirky moments and sandy spills,
Lies the magic of fun under sun-filled thrills.
Beneath the laughter and carefree play,
The essence of joy refuses to stray.

Driftwood Dreams on the Shoreline

I built a castle made of driftwood fine,
But it collapsed quickly, just like my wine.
Where waves whispered secrets to the sand,
I tried to catch crabs with a rubber band.

A parrot squawked my not-so-secret name,
As I danced with locals, oh what a game!
With each step, I risked a new fall,
Attempting the limbo—oh, not at all.

The sand was hot; my feet ran amok,
While seashells giggled, oh what a shock!
I found my shades wedged in a clam,
Wearing them proudly, oh yes, I am glam.

At sunset we sat, drinks clinking bright,
Swapping tall tales 'bout our braver flight.
Each laugh echoed through the calming night,
In driftwood dreams, everything feels right.

Tides of Tranquility

The tide's a tease, pulls back and forth,
As I tried to catch it, oh what a smirk!
With a bucket of shells, I waddled around,
Only to find, mud was my new crown.

A dolphin danced, made a splash and a wink,
While I floundered about trying not to sink.
The beach umbrella was my only shade,
But it rolled away—oh dear, I was played!

My snack of chips turned to seagull bait,
As I waved goodbye to my crisp dinner fate.
In the chaos of laughter, we found our peace,
Tides of tranquility never do cease.

With waves that crashed and giggles that soared,
Our hearts were light, happiness roared.
So let's toast to chaos, at the edge of the sea,
Where silly moments are wild and free.

Laughter in the Saltwater Air

The beach ball soared like a rocket in flight,
But hit Aunt Sally—what a comical sight!
Sand stuck in sunscreen, an artful design,
As we built a pizza from crust and brine.

The sun set low, the sky a wild hue,
We sang silly songs, tried our best to woo.
With toes in the water and laughter so loud,
We danced like the wind, feeling oh-so-proud.

A hammock beckoned, but I missed the cue,
And ended up tangled like a fish out of glue.
Our laughter echoed with a joy so rare,
Creating memories in the saltwater air.

As night wrapped us in its velvety coat,
We shared stories that made our hearts float.
In those funny moments, forever we'll stay,
In laughter and joy, come what may.

Lost in the Embrace of Salt and Sea

Sandy toes with seashells stuck,
I tripped on a wave, oh what luck!
Seagulls laughed as I took a dive,
Splashing around like I'm barely alive.

A cocktail in hand, but it slipped,
Right into the drink, I fully tipped.
Mermaids giggle at my clumsy plight,
While sunburned tourists squint in the light.

Beach volleyball? I gave it a try,
But my serve went high, up to the sky.
It landed on someone's sunbathing head,
Now they're charging me for ice packs instead.

As sunset paints all in hues of gold,
I search for snacks, my hunger bold.
But find the cooler is empty, alas!
Guess I'll feast on my regrets and some grass.

Sun-kissed Horizons and Dreamy Escapes

My flip-flops squeaked with every step,
As I wandered a path, oh what a prep!
Stepped on a crab, he danced like a pro,
But I ran like the wind; it was quite the show.

Watermelon juice dripped down my chin,
A race with a seagull, who'd surely win.
I waved goodbye as it stole my snack,
The seaside thief, never looking back.

A hammock hung like a giggling kid,
I tried to nap, but I couldn't mid.
It swung like a ride, and then I fell,
Now I'm tangled, oh what a tale to tell!

Even the coconut laughed, what a sight!
With a straw like a sword, I drank late at night.
And the moon winked down, all hooting with glee,
Such fun mischief among you and me.

Tales Told by the Driftwood

Driftwood whispers secrets of the sea,
Like a gossiping friend, just for me.
It tells of a crab that danced on the shore,
I swear I saw it, oh, I want more!

Salty breezes poke at my hair,
I wore my hat, but it flew in the air.
Chasing it down was a wild hare's dream,
Fell flat on my face in a sticky ice cream.

A treasure map drawn with a crab's claw,
Led me to nowhere, I must draw the flaw.
But under the stars, I laughed at my luck,
For finding lost laughs beats gold, by a truck.

With a driftwood muse and sand on my feet,
I tell the waves of my win-some defeat,
So every splash, every giggle and cheer,
Will echo my name for all of the year.

Dance of Feathers and Waves

As I danced with a parrot, it squawked in delight,
We twisted and twirled, oh what a sight!
My dance moves clumsy, the bird on my head,
Turning the beach into a circus of red.

The waves tried to join, a splashy romance,
But they tripped on my toes, no chance for a chance.
Together we swayed, a hilariously mess,
Even the sun rolled its rays in distress.

A conga line formed with seashells in hand,
With tourists unsure of which way to stand.
The crab clapped along, with a pinch here and there,
While fish flipped above, winning all the flair.

With a sunset of giggles and promises bright,
I'll dance with the seagulls, from morning till night.
For every shuffle, every wave, and each breeze,
Is a silly reminder of joyful, sweet ease.

Hidden Coves and Echoing Laughter

In a cove where seagulls squawk,
We lost our snacks to a hungry flock.
With sunburned noses and silly grins,
We laughed so hard, we nearly fell in.

A crab danced by, with moves so slick,
His tiny claws clicked—a real party trick.
We joined the crabs in a silly parade,
Waving our arms, not a plan was made.

The tide rolled in and stole our shoes,
We chased the waves, nothing to lose.
With salty hair and splashes loud,
We claimed that beach, it's ours, we're proud!

As the sun dipped low, a nap we sought,
But shells were our pillows, oh, what a lot!
We snored to the symphony of the sea,
Of hidden coves where we live so free.

Barefoot in the Warm Sands

Barefoot we trod on the golden shore,
Each grain of sand was a tickle galore.
We did the twist, fell into a heap,
With waves laughing too, oh what a sweep!

A picnic planned, but oh dear me,
The sandwich flew, carried off by a bee!
We waved our arms, made a crazy dance,
Who knew lunch could lead to such a chance?

Collecting shells, oh what a sight!
They played tricks—one was too tight!
It clung to my foot, wouldn't let go,
I hopped and yelped, a funny show!

As the sun set, we toasted with juice,
Pretending our drinks were full of loose moose.
We giggled at crabs who joined in the fun,
Barefoot adventures, all said and done!

Cabana Nights and Moonlit Tales

Under a cabana, with stars so bright,
We grilled up laughter late into the night.
The barbecue sizzled, smoke in my eye,
With every puff, I thought I might cry!

A coconut fell with a thud and a roll,
Knocking my drink right out of its bowl.
We donned raincoats for a silly toast,
Wishing to drown out our fears like a ghost!

A ukulele played, its strings went twang,
We composed a tune about the wrong slang.
The night was filled with rhymes so bizarre,
Each verse was crazy, we raised each jar!

When the moon took charge, the shadows did prance,
We danced like monkeys in a strange kind of trance.
And when we woke, to our surprise,
The cabana was gone, it took off to the skies!

Captured by the Coral Reef

In the shallows we splashed, feeling so brave,
Silly sea turtles were all we could save.
They played tag with fish, oh what a sight,
While we flailed about, trying to take flight!

A snorkel mishap, I swallowed a wave,
Out came the bubbles, like a silly cave.
A fish gave me side-eye, its gaze was bold,
'You're not a mermaid,' I could hear it scold!

With masks on tight, we searched for treasure,
Only found sunburn, not much to measure.
We laughed at our theories of what we might find,
Gold doubloons? No! Just some long lost rind!

As the tide pulled back, we waved goodnight,
To starfish and conchs, oh what a delight.
Captured by joy in the reef's soft embrace,
With giggles and splashes, we left our trace.

A Whirlwind of Exotic Fragrance

Pineapple hats on sunburned heads,
Coconuts rolling, as laughter spreads.
Flip-flops flying, socks on the run,
Who knew vacation could be this fun?

Margarita spills like a painter's swipe,
Seagulls swooping, they dive and gripe.
Beach chairs tangled, a game of chess,
Amidst the chaos, we just laugh no less.

Sunscreen battles, the spray goes wide,
Our sandy dog makes a perfect slide.
With every splash, a brand new splat,
Oh, the joy of the beachy combat!

As evening falls, we roast marshmallows bright,
Telling tales under the starlit night.
In every blunder, we'll find delight,
This trip's one for the book, that's right!

Chasing Shadows on Golden Sands

Chasing shadows in flip-flop style,
Dodging the waves, all the while.
Kites in the air, tangled with hair,
Life on the shore, who can find a care?

Sunscreen tussles lead to funny burns,
With every wave, our laughter churns.
Turtles and crabs join our wild parade,
We dance to the beat, our own serenade.

Sandcastles built, a little too tall,
Watch them crumble, we loudly enthrall.
Waves laughing back, they play their game,
What's lost to the sea? We can't lay the blame.

Twilight's glow, the BBQ sizzles,
Our taste buds dance as the fire tickles.
With friends by our side, we toast the fun,
Worry, like the tide, will soon be undone!

Lullabies of the Ocean's Caress

Waves whisper softly, tickling our toes,
Sand that clings, oh, where did it go?
Umbrella drinks and an occasional splash,
In this life, we rush but never dash.

Seagulls squawking, claiming their right,
While we dig in, what a silly sight!
Heat in the air, but cold drinks in hand,
So many giggles in this sun-kissed land.

We plan a big trip on a rusty old boat,
But a crab steals the snack, and our hopes start to float.
With comedy here, who needs a show?
With ocean lullabies, we'll just let go.

Sunset comedies end the day right,
With fireflies winking, it's pure delight.
With friends and some snacks, we'll giggle and sway,
Tomorrow's mishaps will just come to play!

Beyond the Breakers and Beyond

Beyond the breakers, our dreams take flight,
Where the sun paints gold at the edge of night.
Sand in our toes, and the sky's in a whirl,
Find me chasing the tide, watch my hair curl.

Catch the coconut, just like a game,
All the local kids shout my name.
The tide pulls back with a cheeky grin,
Where did our snacks go? Oh, let the chase begin!

Sunset picnics become quite a mess,
Chips in the surf, it's anyone's guess.
We miscount our drinks, and someone barters,
What fortune in splashes, amidst all the starters!

So raise a toast to the mischief we find,
With cocktails in plastic, it's fun, every kind.
Beyond the horizon, our laughter will roar,
Life's a beach party, who could ask for more?

When the Ocean Calls

I packed my bags, but forgot my shoes,
The tide rolled in, playing tricks like a muse.
Flip-flops on the wrong feet, I take a stroll,
Seagulls laugh at my landlocked control.

With sunscreen slathered, I look like a ghost,
I try to blend in, but the beach is a host.
Umbrellas are flying, a chaotic parade,
While I'm stuck in sand, too proud to escapade.

A crab pinches my toe, I let out a shriek,
While beachgoers chuckle, I feel so antique.
I dance like a robot, awkward and fun,
Who knew salty air would turn me to pun?

But laughter rings out, and soon I can start,
In this silly circus, I play a fine part.
When the ocean calls, my worries set sail,
For a humorous journey, I've found my true trail.

A Sanctuary of Serenity

In a cozy cabana, I sip on my brew,
Relaxation awaits, but my wifi won't do.
With the sound of the waves, I'm starting to nap,
Until I hear splashes — oh, what's that mishap?

A kid on a floaty, now lost in the tide,
Parents are panicking, oh, such a wild ride!
Their sunscreen's a mess, they've painted the scene,
With more stripes on their faces than any raccoon seen.

I twiddle my toes, feeling sandy and fine,
Only to notice a bee in my wine.
As I swat at the critter, I spill on my hat,
Then laugh as it bumbles away with a spat.

Yet still I relax, for it's all in good cheer,
This sanctuary's magic, it draws me near.
Though chaos surrounds me, I wouldn't retreat,
For laughter and joy can't be beat on this seat.

Embracing the Sun-Soaked Blues

Under a sun that's so bold and so bright,
I put on my shades, but they twist in delight.
My cocktail is melting, it slips from my grip,
And jumps in the pool with a splish and a sip.

A floaty so grand, I jump on with glee,
Then flip upside down, like a fish, oh woe me!
With my legs in the air, I can't help but laugh,
As kids swim on by, giving me the "giraffe."

The lifeguard is laughing, she shakes her sun hat,
As she thinks of the stories of folks who fall flat.
The beach bum beside me just rolls with the tide,
Taking selfies with seagulls, his patience is tried.

Yet here in the chaos, I cherish the thrill,
The sun-soaked blues bring a joy that won't chill.
With whimsies and giggles, the troubles are few,
In this carnival life, let the laughter ensue!

Blossoms of Hibiscus in the Wind

Hibiscus flowers dance in the breeze,
With colors so bright, they simply aim to please.
I tripped in the garden, fell right on my face,
But the flowers don't judge, they just flutter with grace.

A parrot named Percy just stole my hat,
The locals all cheer, while I fume like a brat.
I chase him around, oh what a tough feat,
While he squawks out my secrets — am I really that sweet?

The coconut vendor is rolling his eyes,
As I plead with a bird for my treasure, oh why?
"Sharing is winning!" I call out in jest,
While he flies up high, leaving me in distress.

Yet there in my folly, I find all the cheer,
These blooms tell a story, so vibrant, so clear.
With laughter like petals, they're carried away,
In a whirlwind of joy, forever I'll stay.

www.ingramcontent.com/pod-product-compliance
Lightning Source LLC
Chambersburg PA
CBHW072126070526
44585CB00016B/1556